Powerful Prayers of a Woman on the Altar

Devotionals of a Prayer Warrior

What is an altar? An altar represents a place of consecration. When we surrender our lives to the control of the Holy Spirit, we are lying on the altar of God.

Through many personal trials and victories, I've learned the power of prayer and consecration as a Christian woman. The Lord has shown me what it means and what it takes to be a woman on the altar. It means denying your flesh, taking up your cross daily, and following after Christ. It means standing and trusting God even when life is not making sense at that moment. It means going against your personal judgment and seeking God's guidance and wisdom. Is this an easy thing to do? No, but with God all things are possible. Becoming a woman on the altar comes with maturity and an eagerness for a change in your life. You must get to a place where you are tired of the enemy wreaking havoc in your life and you want to see the promises and power of God fulfilled and displayed in your life.

We, as believers, can possess a level of spiritual authority through prayer and fasting. The Enemy does not want us to be in this place of spiritual

 authority. Why? Because there's a supernatural power that comes from the place of consecration. Our fight is not in the realm of flesh and blood, but in the spiritual realm; therefore, our weapons must be spiritual weapons.

This devotional is deeply personal. Many of the topics and prayers are actual prayers and issues I was facing in my life when the Holy Spirit led me to write them down—not knowing that years later I would be putting them in a devotional book and sharing them with other women who might be facing some of the same types of trials. I would like to encourage each and every person who reads this devotional by telling you to trust the process. Every trial, every victory— all serve a greater purpose in your life. If you stand on the Word and lean on God, He will lead you to the place of destiny, complete and whole.

You will win,

Lakita Sykes

References

Bible verses are from the King James Version unless otherwise indicated.

Thank You, Jesus! Wow, I can't even believe this devotional has finally happened! Lord, I bless You because You are true to Your Word.

I would like to thank my husband, *Calvin Sr.* Keeping up with me is a full-time job. After all these years, you definitely know how to balance me out. Thank you for spoiling me and loving me even with all my flaws. What we have is special. I love you, bae. May you have the desires of your heart.

To my children, *Calvin Jr., Camren, Caden,* and *Nijiah,* the best kids in the world. God truly blessed me beyond words when He gave you to me. I love you'll so much. You are my greatest achievements. Thank you for your support and patience with your mommy. I still need to make up for a lot of nights of not cooking dinner!

Keep pushing and trusting in Jesus.

To my best cheerleader and supporter—and the ultimate woman on the altar. Mommy, I love you!

You spoke out of obedience into my life. You are my role model, a virtuous woman, and a rare, precious gem.

To the greatest dad and pastor this side of heaven! I love your passion for family and for all of God's people. You pour out your heart in words and deeds to anyone who is available to hear and receive. Thank you for always believing in me. I never had to question my place in your heart.

To my baby sister, Amare! Hey, yes, pretty girls do rock for Jesus. I love you. Keep shining. Thank you for your encouragement.

Thank you to all of my physical family, my Battlefield family, and my friends for your encouragement, love, and support.

Lakita Sykes

Day 1

Topic: Shame

Scripture: Romans 8:1, "There is therefore now no condemnation to them which are in Christ Jesus, who walk not after the flesh, but after the Spirit."

For many years I was ashamed of my past, embarrassed by my immaturity and failures. I was even embarrassed by many of the trials and tribulations I had to face. I felt like I was the only one who battled rejection, poverty, mental illness, and the list goes on. But one day while in prayer, the Lord spoke to me very clearly. He said to "tell it." Tell others what makes you a WOTA (Woman on the Altar); tell them what you have been through and have overcome. This is not for you but for others. We need to realize that our testimonies are examples of hope to others facing similar trails. What you have gone through, someone else sitting right next to you could be going through the same battle. They could be on the verge of giving up on life, but you sharing your story of how God brought you out can give that person new hope and the courage not to give up. If He brought you out, He can bring them out. Do you see how it works? We are all here for each other. What you had to face, what you had to endure, was not just for you but for someone else to be delivered.

God's Word tells us in Revelation 12:11, "And they overcame him by the blood of the Lamb, and by the word of their testimony." So the next time the Enemy tries to shame you about your past, remember that your past is the key to unlock someone's current prison. Tell it and silence the Enemy. No more shame!

Prayer: Lord, deliver me from the grips of shame. Give me boldness to share what You have done in my life, the many hills and valleys You have brought me over and through. I want to be a blessing to those who are facing hard times and need hope to keep going. Your word tells me that many are the afflictions of the righteous but the Lord will deliver us out of them all. In Jesus's name, amen.

Day 2

Topic: Finances

Scripture: Philippians 4:19, "But my God shall supply all your need according to his riches in glory by Christ Jesus."

After I became a born again Christian, I was taught that when you're going through financial hardships, you should live according to Matthew 6:33: "But seek ye first the kingdom of God, and his righteousness; and all these things shall be added unto you." While that is true, I believe a closed mouth won't get fed. The Word tells us that life and death lies in the power of the tongue. It wasn't until a few years ago that I realized I have the power and authority through Christ Jesus to decree a thing, and it shall be established. I began to open my mouth and decree financial favor in my life. I would declare the Word of God into the atmosphere daily. Before I knew it, God began to honor His Word, and I began to see a shift in my finances. It is God's good pleasure to bless His people. His Word tells us that He came that we might have life and have it more abundantly. God wants to see His people walking in the abundance of life. Don't you dare believe that He wants to see you lacking and struggling. The devil is a liar. It's time to open your mouth and shift the atmosphere. When the praises go up, the blessings come down.

Prayer: Lord, Your Word tells us that we are the head and not the tail, above and not beneath, lenders and not borrowers. Lord, from this day forth I will trust Your Word. I will open my mouth and declare Your Word over my life and over my finances. I command, in the name of Jesus, every financial blessing that belongs to me and my family to come forth. I decree that I'm walking in an abundance of overflow and prosperity. No more lacking. In Jesus's name, amen.

Day 3

Topic: Healing

Scripture: Isaiah 53:5, "But he was wounded for our transgressions, he was bruised for our iniquities: the chastisement for our peace was upon him; and with his stripes we are healed."

We live in a fractured creation as a result of the fall in the garden of Eden. I often hear people ask what kind of God would want to see His people suffering from sickness and disease. Suffering was never God's intent for His people. This was brought on by sin. For the Word tells us in Romans 6:23 that the wages of sin is death, but the gift of God is eternal life through Christ Jesus. The good news is that we have the victory over sickness through Christ Jesus! Yes, you can really be healed, delivered, and made free. The Word tells us in Matthew 18:18: "Whatsoever ye shall bind on earth shall be bound in heaven: and whatsoever ye shall loose on earth shall be loosed in heaven." I dare you to bind sickness and loose your healing in Jesus's name. The key to receiving your healing is to receive it by faith.

Prayer: Thank you, Lord, for the victory over sickness and disease. I pray that You will heal my body from the crown of my head to the sole of my feet. I pray for a complete healing in my body and that everything will line up and function the way You have created it to function. Lord, perform a supernatural miracle in my body today. In the mighty, matchless name of Jesus, amen.

Day 4

Topic: Fear

Scripture: 2 Timothy 1:7, "For God hath not given us the spirit of fear; but of power, and of love, and of a sound mind."

We have all dealt with fear, experiencing it in one way, shape, form, or another in our lives. Fear is being afraid of someone or something, to be fearful, scared, apprehensive, or terrified. When we give in to fear, we're giving the person or thing we fear power over us. God's Word clearly says that He has given us power! It's time for us to take back our power from the spirit of fear. I often call fear a spiritual flesh-eating disease; daily it eats away at our hope and dreams. Fear is a vision thief and a dream killer. It keeps you locked up spiritually, afraid to step out and trust God. We're fearful of what others will think about us, fearful of trying and failing. Before you know it, you have completely let fear cripple you and talk you out of what God has for you. But not anymore. Today I serve notice to fear: your days of tormenting me are over. I am more than a

conqueror through Christ Jesus. In Jesus's name, I'm coming for
everything the enemy said I couldn't have.

Prayer: Today, Lord, I praise You and thank You for the victory over fear.
No longer will I be scared, apprehensive, and crippled by the tricks and
devices of the enemy. I speak Your word over this spirit. Your Word tells
me in 1 John 4:18, "…perfect love casteth out fear." I have been given
power, love, and a sound mind. I will walk this day forward in spiritual
authority and victory over fear in Jesus's name.

Day 5

Topic: Guidance

Scripture: Proverbs 3:5-6, "Trust in the LORD with all thine heart; and lean not unto your own understanding. In all thy ways acknowledge him, and he shall direct thy paths."

Have you ever desperately wanted something or wanted to do something? Perhaps a job, a spouse, a new car, or to relocate. I mean, you prayed about it. You sought the Lord for direction—only to get no answer or not the answer you wanted. But because you wanted it so badly and because you were leaning to your own understanding about the matter, you disregarded all of the red flags. You disregarded God's no, and you went for it anyway. And boy, when you got what you had asked for, you eventually found out why God didn't want you to have it. We have to learn to trust God's timing and His perfect will for our lives. Often we can save ourselves heartache, disappointments, and setbacks if we will just wait on God and let Him order our steps. We live in a microwave society. We just got to have it now! There's no patience or discipline within us to encourage us to wait and trust God for what's best. God sees the big picture, and we're only looking through a small crack. He sees what's up the road ahead and does not want us to endure many of the mishaps we will end up facing if we take that path. But the good news is, He is still with us even when we fall short. We just need to get up, dust ourselves off, and get back in the race—this time giving Him complete control to lead and guide us.

Prayer: Lord, thank You for Your grace and mercy. Even when I step out of Your will for my life, You're still there and ready to give me another chance to get it right. I pray today that You will help me to put my trust in You. You tell me in Jeremiah 29:11 that You know the plans You have for me. They are good plans and not evil, to give me hope and a future. Lord, where You lead me, I will follow. In Jesus's name, amen.

Day 6

Topic: Rejection

Scripture: Psalm 27:10, "When my father and my mother forsake me, then the LORD will take me up."

I remember standing at the payphone with my mother at the age of seven years old. Even as a child, I had enough sense to know that my Mom was hurt beyond words. "What do you mean she's not your child after seven years?" After listening to a heated argument between my mother and my father, I became confused and hurt, wondering why my dad would not want to see me anymore? A seed was planted from this experience; I didn't realize it at that time. But it would take many years for me to be delivered from the spirit of rejection and abandonment. Rejection is a very real hurt that often comes from our childhood. Being abandon or unloved many times opens the door to the spirit of rejection. Once I became a born again believer and gave my life to the Lord, He began to heal me from the hurt of rejection. He also began to show me in numerous ways how others' rejection was God's way of protecting me and the call that was on my life. So yes, God will block somethings in your life. Yes, you will be rejected by others in this walk. Will it hurt? Yes. But we know that God's Word teaches that all things work together for the good of them that love the Lord and those who are called according to His purpose. Amen.

Prayer: Lord, I thank You for protecting me, even though it may hurt when others reject me. I know You see my future and what's best for my life. Lord, I pray that You will heal and deliver me from the need to always be accepted by others. Help me learn to trust and discern who You want in my life and to accept Your decisions about who should not be in my life. Your Word teaches me in Psalm 32:8 that You will guide me along the best pathway for my life. You will advise me and watch over me. I thank You for watching over me. In Jesus's name, amen.

Day 7

Topic: Forgiveness

Scripture: Proverbs 10:12, "Hatred stirreth up strifes: but love covereth all sins."

Bitterness is the state in which human beings find themselves when they cannot let go and let God or when they are unable to fully forgive others. I've learned that unforgiveness is another gateway for the enemy to enter. Unforgiveness sits in your heart, and if it's not dealt with and cast out, it will block and hinder you from moving forward. You'll begin to harbor resentment and anger.

Power is not found in holding on to unforgiveness; power is in being able to release and let go of your hurt so that you can move on in peace. Unforgiveness is a trick of the enemy, used to keep you bookmarked in hurt and in the past. But when you let go and let God, you're able to move to the next page and chapter in your life. There's victory for you in forgiving. Amen.

Prayer: Lord, I know Your Word tells me in Matthew 6:14-15 that I must forgive others in order to receive Your forgiveness. Lord, I pray that You will help me and strengthen me to forgive. Deliver me from the hurt, disappoint, and betrayal of others. I want to be free and at peace in my heart and mind. Create in me a clean heart and renew my spirit. In Jesus's name, amen.

Day 8

Topic: Faith

Scripture: Hebrews 11:1, "Now faith is the substance of things hoped for, and the evidence of things not seen."

As believers, our entire walk with God is built on faith. We serve and believe in Him, yet we have never seen Him. But we believe by faith that He is real and so is His word. That could be why His Word tells us in Hebrews 11:6 that without faith it's impossible to please God. We don't know exactly how powerful our faith is. Our faith in God and His Word has the ability to bring forth healing, deliverance, breakthrough, miracles, signs, and wonders, and the list goes on. The Word also tells us that life and death are in the power of our own tongue. Wow, that means I have the power to speak and decree the blessings of God over my life and the lives of my family! I encourage you to open your mouth and begin to pray and ask for the Lord's blessings in faith. Amen.

Prayer: Lord, Your Word tells me in Mark 11:24 that when I pray, believing that I have already received it, it shall be mine. Lord, I thank You for increasing my faith. I speak Your blessings in faith over me and my family. I thank You for giving me faith that can move mountains. In Jesus's name, amen.

Day 9

Topic: Patience

Scripture: James 1:4, "But let patience have her perfect work, that ye may be perfect and entire, wanting nothing."

What do you do when God has made you a promise, which has been prophesied and confirmed, but here you are weeks, months, or years later and nothing has happened? The promise may be for a soulmate, healing, financial breakthrough, salvation for unsaved loved ones, etc. I've learned that there's a process to receiving God's promises for your life. It's not that God doesn't want to bless you; it's actually His desire to see you blessed and prosperous. His Word tells us in 3 John 1:2 that above all things He wants us to prosper and be in good health even as our soul prospers. But there's a time and a season for all things. What we may be seeking and asking God for may not line up with His timetable. The good news is that delay is not denial. We sometimes aren't ready for certain things, and God has to take us through a season of preparation, where He processes and prepare us for the blessings and manifestations to come. The preparation season is to teach us how to walk into the blessing, how to treat it, and how to be a good steward over it. So whatever the promise, whether a godly mate, a new home, or a prosperous business, let patience have her perfect work in you and through you. Amen.

Prayer: Lord, I praise You and thank You for taking me through the process of preparation. I thank You for preparing me for a greater blessing, because I know it's coming. You said in Your

Word in 1 Corinthians 2:9, "Eye hath not seen, nor ear heard, neither have entered into the heart of man, the things which God hath prepared for them that love him." I asked that you help me to not be weary while I wait. In Jesus Name. Amen.

Day 10

Topic: Loneliness

Scripture: Hebrews 13:5, "Let your conversation be without covetousness; and be content with such things as ye have: for he hath said, I will never leave thee, nor forsake thee."

Have you ever been in a room with many people, but you still felt alone? Like no one there understood what you were feeling or going through? Maybe your loneliness is due to a lack of companions or a lonely spirit. Being lonely is hard. How do I know? Because I have been there. Just a few years ago, my storms had me in a place of social isolation and loneliness. I felt like people didn't understand what I was going through; they didn't know the pain I was feeling. I couldn't talk to anyone; it was just too much. But the Lord reminded me what His Word says in 1 Peter 5:7: "Casting all my care upon him; for he cares for you." I want you to know that you are not alone, and God sees you exactly where you are. He is with you through the storms, seeing you through every difficult and lonely season in your life. Let His presence be the strength you need to get through. He promises never to leave you nor forsake you. Amen.

Prayer: Father, I know Your Word tells me to be strong and courageous because You are with me wherever I go. Lord, I pray that You will surround me with Your peace and comfort in times of trouble that I may have strength in knowing that You are with me in the midst of it all. In Jesus's name, amen.

Day 11

Topic: Depression

Scripture: Isaiah 41:10 (NIV), "So do not fear, for I am with you; do not be dismayed, for I am your God. I will strengthen you and help you; I will uphold you with my righteous right hand."

We live in a society today where everyone is comparing and measuring their success and failures against those of the next person. Often this happens through social media. Comparing our successes and failures with the next person's is a trick from the enemy and leads many into the spirit of depression. You find yourself having a pity party because your life is not where someone else's is. Do not get caught up in comparison; work with what you have to the best of your ability. Your house may not be the biggest, your income may not be six figures, or you may not yet be married. The apostle Paul says it best in Philippians 4:11: "…for I have learned, in whatsoever state I am, therewith to be content." I encourage you, my sister, to be faithful over the small, and God will bless you with the increase.

Prayer: Lord, I pray that You will help me to be faithful in my current condition. Help me not to get caught up in the spirit of comparison that can lead down paths of depression and unhappiness. I plead the blood of Jesus over my thoughts. I pray for a spirit of gratefulness to be upon me. I know that Your Word says "to everything there is a season, and a time." Help me to wait patiently on my time and change to come. In Jesus's name, amen.

Day 12

Topic: Joy

Scripture: Nehemiah 8:10b (NIV), "Do not grieve, for the joy of the LORD is your strength."

Has there been a time in your life when nothing was wrong, and everything was actually going well? However, deep down on the inside, you were still not at peace. You may have been happy, but something was still missing. But when you have joy, you are filled with peace and contentment. You won't find this peace and contentment in money, material possessions, or people. Only God can fill you with His joy. His Word tells us in Psalm 16:11b: "in thy presence is fullness and joy; at thy right hand there are pleasures for evermore." Happiness is great, but it is also contingent upon what's going on around you or how you feel. I would rather have joy from the Lord because you can have joy even when you may be dealing with a storm. You can still be at peace. Why? Because the joy of the Lord is the strength you need to make it through.

Prayer: I bless you, Lord, for this is the day that You have made; I will rejoice and be glad in it. You tell me in Your word that weeping may endure for a night, but joy comes in the morning. Lord, help me to be of good cheer and to have joy unspeakable, no matter what may be going on around me. Thank you for your joy. In Jesus's name, amen.

Day 13

Topic: Grief

Scripture: Matthew 5:4 (NIV), "Blessed are those who mourn, for they will be comforted."

Losing a loved one is hard. No doubt, it is one of the hardest things we face in life. My family went through a season of death and grieving where we were hit with one death after another. I was overwhelmed and found myself in deep grief, experiencing a spectrum of emotions: shock, disbelief, fear, anxiety, and anger, to name a few. The hurt was unreal and at times unbearable. I became confused and needed answers. There was no relief to be found until I let go and completely surrendered to God, crying out and sobbing, "God, I need you!" He then began to comfort and minister to me through His Word, reminding me that this world is not our home, and we're just passing through. Does it hurt to see the ones we love so dearly pass on? Yes, it hurts. God knows it hurt. He tells us in Psalm 46:1-2 that He is our refuge and strength, a very present help in the time of trouble. Trust God for your healing in times of grief.

Prayer: Lord, Your Word tells me to cast all my cares upon You because You care for me. Lord, I need You to help and heal my heart from this hurt. Lord, give me strength to go on. I trust that every day You will take a little more pain from my heart. I know that earth has no sorrow that heaven cannot heal. Help me not to get stuck in grief. Close the doors that will allow depression and anxiety to enter. In Jesus's name, amen.

Day 14

Topic: Purpose

Scripture: Jeremiah 29:11, "For I know the plans that I have for you,' declares the LORD, plans to prosper you and not to harm you, plans to give you hope and a future."

Lord, what is my purpose? What am I here to do? Do you ever find yourself asking God those questions? I have; however, it wasn't until I was in my thirties that I finally began to understand my purpose here on earth. I spent so much time chasing what I thought was purpose and operating on my own will. You won't truly know your purpose in life until you lay down your will and let God's will be done in you. I spent years seeking fulfillment through jobs and other ordinary pursuits. But God said, "I didn't call you to be ordinary. I called you to preach the good news, to encourage, uplift, and restore those in need with my Word." Your purpose is your reason for being on this earth. It could be teaching children or serving as a missionary, doctor, or pastor. Purpose is the one thing that's bigger than you and leaves you fulfilled because you know it's God-ordained. Walk out your purpose with faith and boldness.

Prayer: Thank you, Lord, for being the author and finisher of my life. Your Word tells me in Psalms 37:23 that "the steps of a good man are ordered by the Lord." God, lead my steps; guide me into my purpose in life. Let Your will be done in me and through me. I lay my life down at Your feet, and I trust Your plans for me. In Jesus's name, amen.

Day 15

Topic: Deliverance

Scripture: Psalm 34:17 (NIV), "The righteous cry out, and the LORD hears them; he delivers them from all their troubles."

When a person is battling an alcohol or drug addiction, one of the first steps for getting help is to first admit or acknowledge that he or she has an issue. If an addict is in denial, chances are the addict will stay in the problem and remain bound to it. But when a person becomes sick and tired of being in bondage to drug addictions, abusive relationships, poverty, and generational curses, that's when God can move. Deliverance comes when we no longer enjoy the bondage of our problems, when we say, "Lord, I need a change in my life. I no longer enjoy being in this toxic relationship (or I no longer enjoy being in debt or I no longer enjoy <u>whatever our problem is</u>)." What you just did was identified the problem in your life and released it to God for Him to handle. That's the formula for deliverance: identify the problem, release it to God, and don't turn back. Amen.

Prayer: Lord, You are my very present help in the time of trouble. I thank You for being my way maker and my deliverer. I believe Your Word that tells me, "If the Son therefore shall make you free, ye shall be free indeed." Kill any pride in me that would block me from surrendering and finding complete deliverance. I plead the blood of Jesus over my life and over anything that has held me in bondage. I receive my deliverance today in Jesus name, amen.

Day 16

Topic: Marriage

Scripture: Mark 10:9 (NIV), "What God has joined together, let no one separate."

Being married for 17 years has taught me a lot. I have learned that nothing tries the foundation of a marriage like financial issues and outside influences. The enemy definitely uses these tools to drive a wedge between a husband and a wife. Financial stress can steal the peace in a home; it brings frustration and division. Outside influences are another tool that the enemy uses to bring confusion into a marriage. It's so important for a husband and wife to remember they're on the same team. Communicate in love and respect. Apologize often, learn to forgive, and kill your pride. Learn to build a wall around your union; guard it and protect it. Also protect your privacy and your peace. The enemy can use anyone, including family, to destroy your union. I'll say that again: the enemy can use anyone—including family. As a woman on the altar, it's not always a good idea to vent your marriage issues to family members or friends. We must use great discernment when doing so. If we truly want to see great results and complete victory, we must learn to take our marriage to the Lord in prayer. Be at peace and know that prayer is your weapon, and it can change your marriage for the best. Amen.

Prayer: Thank you, Lord, for my husband. Lord, help me to honor him and my vows to him. Lord, help me to be a blessing and not a hindrance to him. Help him to be a blessing to me and to love me as Christ loved the church. Your Word asks how two can walk together if they are not in agreement. Strengthen our communication and restore, renew, and revive the places in our marriage that are lacking. I decree victory and prosperity over our union. Lord, block all negative outside influences. In Jesus's name, amen.

Day 17

Topic: Children

Scripture: Proverbs 22:6, "Train up a child in the way he should go: and when he is old, he will not depart from it."

Being a mother of four has truly been one of the best things I have accomplished on this earth. Every pregnancy, labor, and delivery has all been worth the joy that being a mother brings. The joy of watching my children take their first steps, attend their first day of school, and achieve their highest accomplishments is unsurpassed, creating priceless memories. Oftentimes, when looking at the condition of our world and the times we're living in, I find myself experiencing moments of anxiety and worry over them. With all the school shootings, drugs, gang activities, and so much more going on in our world, it's hard to release our kids from our grip. My oldest son now has friends who are driving, and he'll soon be driving also. Every time he asks me if he can hang out with his friends, my first thought

is to say no. But I know I must let him grow up. This does not mean allowing him to do anything he wants but giving him a little rope. I have to trust him with going to the mall or the movies with his friends, to trust that he will be mature and responsible. I used to find myself praying with tears in my eyes. *Lord, did I do everything right by my children? Lord, did I teach them what I should have? Will they make the right choices in the face of peer pressure?* In those moments, the Lord let me know His answer: *Yes, you did right by them. You trained them up in Me from birth. Now let them walk out their own journey.* We as mothers will have to loosen our grips eventually and trust that the Lord has our children in His care. We may loosen our grip, but never our prayers over their lives. Amen.

Prayer: Lord, thank You for blessing me with my children. I pray that You will give me the strength to trust that they're in Your hands. I pray that You will continue to cover them and protect them. I plead the blood of Jesus over them and decree that no weapon formed against them shall be able to prosper. I declare Your favor and blessings upon them and upon everything they do in life. In Jesus's name, amen.

Day 18

Topic: Love

Scripture: 1 Corinthians 13:4 (NIV), "Love is patient, love is kind. It does not envy, it does not boast, it is not proud."

When I read about the kind of love described in 1 Corinthians 13:4, I think about my Lord and Savior Jesus Christ. He had so much love for us that He willingly laid down his life. We didn't deserve it; we couldn't earn it because the price was too high for us to pay. Now think about how many times we have refused to forgive or even have dealings with people because we felt like they didn't deserve our presence or our love. I know I'm guilty too. It's so easy for us to get caught up in our fleshly feelings and not love each other as Christ has commanded us to. Does this type of love come overnight? Of course not. But as you continue to grow in your spiritual walk with Christ and lay down every weight and sin at the altar, God will grow you to walk in an unconditional agape love for others. There is no way as believers in Christ that we can have a prayer life and the Holy Spirit but not real love for our brothers and sisters. 1 John 4:20 (NKJV) says, "If someone says, 'I love God' and hates his brother, he is a liar." You cannot fake love, and you cannot fool God. He knows our hearts. If you're finding yourself struggling to truly love others for whatever reason, I encourage you to seek God for healing and deliverance. Jesus is love. Amen.

Prayer: Lord, I love You because You first loved me. In return, help me to share that same love with others. Lord, if there's anything in me that would stop me from loving others freely, I pray that you will remove it from my heart. I ask that You will create in me a clean heart and renew a right spirit within me. In Jesus's name, amen.

Day 19

Topic: Peace

Scripture: Isaiah 26:3 "Thou will keep him in perfect peace, whose mind is stayed on thee, because he trusteth in thee."

I can recall times in my life when all hell was breaking loose. Everything that could go wrong was going wrong. I remember thinking that if people heard my story, they wouldn't believe it even if I told them it was true. Not that I was perfect or trying to hide it or mask it, but because I had the peace of God which surpasses all understanding, I learned how to put my trust and faith in Him. No matter what I may be facing, I know God is with me, and He will see me through. His Word tells me in Romans 8:28 that all things are working together for my good. God will give you peace in the midst of confusion. God doesn't want us to panic every time trouble comes. He wants us to rest assured in the fact that He is God and He can do anything but fail. Amen.

Prayer: Lord, I need your peace to be upon me. No matter what I may face in my life, I will not grow weary or dismayed. You tell me in Your Word that if I keep my mind on You, You will keep me in perfect peace. Lord, help me to put all my focus on You. Help me to meditate on Your Word day and night. Guard my thoughts and my heart. I put my trust and hope in You. In Jesus's name, amen.

Day 20

Topic: Envy/Jealousy

Scripture: James 3:16, "For where envying and strife is, there is confusion and every evil work."

The Word of God tells us to esteem others better than ourselves; however, we are now living in the times of a "It's all about me, so I can't celebrate the next person" mentality. When I was growing up, my Mom taught me to be confident but not vain, and there is a huge difference. When you are confident in yourself and who God has called you to be, there's no room to harbor envy and jealousy. You can celebrate your sister without being intimidated by her light. But when you're vain and insecure, you will struggle with celebrating others because you feel that their light dims your light. We live in a social media era that promotes vain and self-centered behavior. A lot of these behaviors are fueled by the spirit of comparison, competition, and jealousy. But as women on the altar, there is no place for such behaviors in our hearts. God said in His Word that we are fearfully and wonderfully made. When we stand in Godly confidence, we will be able to celebrate others in love. We must cast down the spirits of envy or jealousy and refuse to operate under their control. Amen.

Prayer: Lord, help me and search me. If You find any envy and jealousy in me, I ask that You remove it. Deal with hidden insecurities that may cause me to be jealous of my sister or brother. Help me not to want what others have, but to be content in my season. I trust Your will for my life. Give me Godly confidence in who You have created me to be. In Jesus's name, amen.

Day 21

Topic: Spiritual Warfare

Scripture: Deuteronomy 28:7, "The LORD will cause your enemies who rise against you to be defeated before your face; they shall come out against you one way and flee before you seven ways."

I spent many years of my life not knowing how much power and authority I had over the enemy. The Lord tells us in Luke 10:19 that He has given us power to tread upon serpents and scorpions and power over the enemy; and nothing shall be able to hurt us. The enemy is already defeated according to the Word of God. It's our job as believers to know that and to operate in our faith and authority. We also should know that Ephesians 6:11 tells us we're not fighting against flesh and blood, but our fight is spiritual. We waste so much time living in our flesh and angry at people when our fight is with the spirit operating through the individuals. We need to aim our prayers at the spirit and hit our target. Then the enemy is exposed and has to flee. And guess what? We walk away with the victory. Amen.

Prayer: Lord, I pray that you will expose every enemy in my life. Reveal the spirit behind every attack or potential attack. I pray for spiritual discernment to see the enemy a mile away. Your Word tells me in 2 Corinthians 10:4 that "the weapons of our warfare are not carnal, but mighty through God to the pulling down of strong holds." I plead the blood of Jesus over me and my family, that no weapon formed against us shall be able to prosper. I am victorious through Christ Jesus. In Jesus's name, amen.

<u>*About the Author*</u>

Woman on the Altar is a vision God has given Evangelist Lakita Sykes. Lakita is an anointed, bold mouthpiece for the Lord. Her passion is preaching, teaching, praying, healing, and bringing deliverance to all of God's people. Through many trials in her own personal life, she has learned the power of praying and standing on the Word of God. She serves her local church (The Battlefield Church of Christ in Norfolk, Virginia) faithfully and diligently. She loves to encourage and support others in love and with the Word of God.

Lakita also coaches and counsels' women in all walks of life, helping them to find their purpose and destiny in the Lord. She's known for her soft voice and bold message: transformation in Christ. A wife and mother, Lakita approaches life with a nurturing and sensitive attitude toward those who are spiritually hurting and crying for help. She's learned that real transformation can take place on the altar of God. One of her favorite Scriptures is Jeremiah 29:11: "For I know the thoughts that I think toward you, saith the LORD, thoughts of peace, and not of evil, to give you an expected end."